# A PRELIMINARY VISION TESTED IN THE FLOWER

## Kenneth Pobo

# CONTENTS

# I. Splits

# A SPLIT MAN

Aaron never challenges the mirror
anymore, turns his head away
from store windows. He's barely
visible in the glass. No, he says—
it's better not to see,
not to have proof.

How do trees growing near ponds
do it?—he wonders. Leaves
finding their own strange
reflection: is that lonely green
one really me?

He believes his image
has a better time than he does.
What fun to disappear
when lights go out, to fade
like a smoke ring in rafters.

He throws his body on the bed,
a sack of sand from which angry
lizards poke out roughened heads
to see moonlight verify them.

# AARON'S DREAMS

In sleep the theatre I am opens.
The patrons are also
in the film. I dreamed I saw
mother making love to a man
with a diamond in his ear, father
beside them, drinking
while they went at it.

Last year mother died.
Dad won't talk about her,
even took their wedding picture
off the wall. Everyone had forgiven her
hundreds of uncommitted sins.

Tonight, a year later,
my fingers split open,
pouring out dreams
which run around the room,
tire and fall asleep. Night

bears golden fruit, bitter,
the tender rind a body I remember
in a still house.

# AARON WAKING

In dreams I become
a thrasher rusting
on a field. I try to recall
how I got here, who ran off
and forgot me. My dead
parents, weeds;
rain runs down
tender shoots.
I dream of them,
wake in a sweat
which I prefer
to not dreaming of them.
Slowly I wake,
unable to move.
Frost on my gears,
years nobody can fix.

# AARON WATCHING DR. FRANK

At nine, Aaron's favorite show
was *Video Village*: hop
from square to square to win
furniture, money, or furs.

After the show, Dr. Frank
gave a five-minute pediatrics
pep talk from a black chair.

When he interviewed a boy
named Andy, he asked him
"Are you usually the first
one picked for softball?"
Andy grinned and said yes,
he was often the captain.

Chosen last, even after
Chuck Daleedan, Aaron
went clammy.

A cereal commercial followed
Dr. Frank. An Andy look-alike
With an angel-food face
ate breakfast. That September
in school, each popular kid
was Andy. Aaron kept his distance.

Twenty years later, Aaron
mistrusts any Andy, the same
guys he often falls for.

# MECHANICAL DRAWING

At the slanted desk
I draw plates, designs
for things I'll never make.
Our teacher demands
silence so we can concentrate,
which I can't do, my clothesline
mind weighted down.
I anger him by hand
drawing lines: ALWAYS
use the ruler,
never free hand. All these

perfectly straight lines,
I'll never fit in them—
I toss the ruler
in Salt Creek. It becomes
the canoe
it really wants to be.

# AARON IN LOVE AT 16

He was never sweet,
not even at sixteen,
though his family called
him an angel.
Angels are sexless
and Aaron was in love
for the first time with
Kirk, who cried whenever
Petula Clark hit the radio.
What more could Aaron
hope for? They took long
walks behind the mall,
spent hours each day
on the phone, explored
each other in under-
construction houses.
Of course, it didn't last.
This was half his life ago—
he wishes Petula Clark
didn't have to pay for
what had disappeared with
shirts he had outgrown.

# FATHER

1.


The Magnificent Mile glitters like a freshly washed pig.
Windy City, lit by various gadgets. Each night we have
Boodles gin martinis. The woman waits at home, prepares
Sunday School lessons and dinner. In fifth grade,
Aaron knows every state capital.

In Illinois is a kind of light I haven't seen elsewhere,
as if farmland is a clear tabletop with tiny candles
burning beneath. With a foot in five decades, five streams,
time is algae between my toes. I am the hotels I build.
My family is a transition, a difference between mist and fog.

2.


Bushes before our porch are green in the instep of dusk.
Susan is in the hospital giving birth: 1951. Our house,
a spider web on a wheel. She was an artist before marriage.
Her body pours another into the city limits. She says,
"I don't feel it anymore, not like I used to." I look
through the window and the window looks back—we shall call
him Aaron, a name with no bend to it.

3.


Kicking leaves off your grave, I, Aaron, indulge your resem-
blance
in my mirror. Five years ago a willow merged with a white stone.

Wind through a willow I want to be... like you, father.
I leave when the sun's yellow top spins out. My bouquet
melts
    memory
        petals.

# ELEGY IN MISERABLE WEATHER

In a windowbox, Mother
grew cornflowers which swept
over her, soft clean wind.

Just days before
she was killed she said:
"Never live alone.
It's hell
living alone.
It's hell
living with someone."

I am my household.
On the card table,
a sherry bottle
stuffed with white
blossoms: odor of cornflowers

crushed in a cedar chest,
odor of stale sherry
in a white kitchen.

# FUNERAL PHOTOGRAPH

In the attic that smell
again newspaper lining walls
headlines 1928 the air around them
heavy as a Swedish forest

A small desk
photos inside ink on their flipsides
barely legible more legible than
those lives now
a farm a general store a Chicago house
Scandinavian yellow and Bavarian purple
the color they form that's me
a spy in my own dark country

 Private moments
of the dead lighter than my hands
then a photo
filled with flowers I wonder
who's getting married look closer
a funeral Oscar shaded by lens and lily
died when I was one between
wife five daughters two sons
went to sleep at a party made his way
to this pile of prints

From the porch comes laughter
I close the desk slip downstairs
and outside stand on the stump
of a cherry tree cut down in 1961
imagining cherries heat-red the smell
 heavy across my lashes

# OL' LADY STERN

Aaron, I'm standing on your lids.
I'm the angel who danced on
the head of the pin-
stripe suit
you wore to Fire Island last year.
You thought nobody saw you?
Behold, I sit at the right hand
of Eleanor Roosevelt, lady
of our labors, rose without end.
I make myself at home in your skull,
a filthy sink
crawling with devils.

I know you never liked me.
You yawned
at my funeral when Father Colter
spoke of a place of peace.
God! He made Heaven
sound like a moldy resale shop!
I saw you checking your watch,
hoping someone would take you
to McDonald's.

At night I'll come to you.
Your lovers
will marvel at your distance.

In the silence after love,
you'll see eyes in the walls,

eyes in the carpet.
Then dear, truly you'll speak
and have nothing to say.

# THERE WAS PERHAPS A PRELIMINARY VISION TESTED IN THE FLOWER

I'd have made a good African
violet shade
on shade purple flowers I remember them
whirling against a lace curtain
a blank smell the orange water can a tipped
flamingo beak whiteness of
my mother's hand at night
slightly stroking the blossoms
she wouldn't let me touch them
they were like altar candles I believed that
each had secret powers
were desert mystics vowing silence
till death a mere chill
could dissolve each wound
after mother died I saw them
dumped in trash petals stained with coffee
grounds and milkshake
I could've killed my grandmother then sailed
off on a red boat sky
hoping Father Colter is right after all
she is just over the rainbow weaving between
stars I looked up
marveling at yellow light emptying
over my shoulders in the garage
a cut root crawling over a cereal box

# AARON, DRIFTING OFF

I fall asleep clutching
 the bed.
 Is each blanket real?
 Faith?
I've always believed
in God, not knowing why,
but liking the notion
if I would die this
very minute, I'd be where
butterflies flex
on my shoulder and music
turns space to a ballroom.

So certain. Even a year ago
the afterlife, valid
as a coffee cup.
The movie ends, that's all,
where else to go but to the exit?

I keep attending
Dilbury Episcopal Church:
the priest, a coloring book
in vestments. Today
I wake at 7:15,
get out the tan suit

Roberta says makes me gaunt,
black squeaky shoes, a light
 brown tie.

A little coffee. Toast.
Then in the car
to drive toward the quiet
before others arrive.

Peace be with you, says Father,
And also with you, I reply
from my oaken space. Alone, here,
 I think, so beautiful this way.

Kyrie Eleison... Kyrie Eleison... Kyrie
 Eleison...
Allelujia... Allelujia... Allelujia...

I kneel by the rail
for the wafer's paper taste,
return to the pew.
Notes slide up to rafters
from a red hymnal. Battered
lips turn soft as violets.
 A cinnamon smell.

Nobody old or young. Melody,
harmony—the dead among us!

Maybe if I'm lucky tonight
I won't fall asleep
clutching the bed.

After shaking
each necessary hand, I
find my car, remember
Susan Hayward in <u>I Want To Live</u>.
The time arrives... no call comes.

Afterwards, I visit Roberta.
I can't go there anymore,
I tell her over spaghetti.

Home again, I take a hot bath.
Water loosens bones,
the soapbar heavy and inquisitive.
A baptism, perhaps, a laying on
of my own hands. In my ears,
mosquitoes, "Jesus loves me,
 this I know...."

 Jesus, Roberta, and Willy Jean
love me, I confide

to the washcloth. I'm turning
into water, my skin's
 already a lake,
my breath, leaves.

Bedtime—the covers, the pillow.
Lying there, drowsy. Dreams
are where it's wonderful,
risking nightmares. Fall.

I'm drifting off. God
will not stop me.
God wants me to sleep
well, perhaps. Sleep
like I'll never awaken.
Is this how it is in the long run?
 No clutching,
just a drifting off,
 a drifting off
 a drifting off

# AARON'S WAY

A gay teenager,
I didn't commit suicide,

though I tried. My folks pulled me
back from the brink,

sent me to church camp,
a youth group, scouts, a shrink.

They put everything in gear
to keep me from "turning

queer," but I never turned,
just was, and now I'm learning

how to make mistakes
and how to love because

joy slipped the noose of despair.
Even when grief aches,

a razor on my backbone,
I remember others share

my pain, my anger. So I
feel less in danger, less alone.

# 1980

Each Saturday Aaron comes
with his friend Eric who says,
"I think of my lovers as meat
at Shop-Rite. I check what's
under the wrapping before
taking it home." If no one

will dance with them, they dance
together to "Rock Lobster" and
"We Are Family." Under
the turning silver ball Aaron stares
at his shoes, scared to make
eye contact, can't see
under the wrapper. Smoked out

in sweaty cologne, they go
home to separate doors,
a spilled brandy of stars
on Frederick Avenue,
love a drumbeat
thumping in Aaron's sleep,

morning's red silk shirt
on the sheet.

# LIKE A FIVE YEAR OLD

In the Montserrat Café
we talk about Etta James,
Tommy James, Henry James,
and several other James's.
Leonard the waiter takes

our order: Jimmy get something
trendy; Aaron gets a burger.
Jimmy says Aaron "simply must stop
eating like a five year old."
Yes, but he likes a good rut—

rarely misses an
*Addams Family* rerun
or a summer's evening
following moths in the field
off Henley Street. Aaron's

no child at heart, not in
love with childhood, a basement
full of spiders. Thursday
night Jimmy didn't consider him
a child. Still, he often needs

to feel safe, as a child does,
and Jimmy makes him feel safe,
loved. Not like Aaron's father,
but as a lover, who holds him,
purrs after making love.

# AARON LOVES

It looks like rain
so he goes to the field.
Ankle-weedy
November breaks
the remaining goldenrod,
blackens the sun's signature.

Why is my life given to gray,
he asks. Some love best
the extremes,
will never believe anything
beautiful if it doesn't
decompose, drop
a leaf inside them
which echoes in the bloodstream.

So thinks Aaron: stump
dancer, eyes
fragile as fallen apples.

# AARON THINKS HE'S A JUKEBOX

His friends stand around him, softly
knocking knuckles on his arms.
They are quarters hunting for the song
which will lead them like a roadmap
to the Cosmic Orgasm, a burst
of inner music,
a hymn that eats you alive.
Buttons pushed, he sets the juice loose.
They want him to be Jesus,
the rock star from Palm Springs.

 At the center
of Aaron's heart, a dark room fills
with the ouch of a mean-tempered drum.
Vampires circle each other inside.
The old fairy guarding Aaron's aorta
hears dance tunes, likes the flashing
white lights of Aaron's ribs, gray
rooftops of the lungs.

Bored by the jukebox selection,
Aaron's friends want to enter this room
to hear the secret song.
They scream into the parade of chords
but Aaron increases the volume.

At closing time when the machine disconnects,
Aaron withdraws alone into the room.
The beautiful dancers are killing
each other, turn their guns on Aaron,
shoot him. He bleeds their silence.

# AARON HOBNOBS

Happy, I have on my favorite
patio shoes, a sleeveless
red shirt and black jeans.
I'm where the brilliant
become martinis and gossip
about last month's kink.
I nod, my neck a pendulum
swinging from name to name.

In a corner, someone
signs book jackets.
Another flips through
a tall, breathing novel.

I always wanted to swim
between shoulder pads
and tweed jackets,

in a room above the city,
talent around my legs,

a tail-up-high tabby.

# EVEN NOW

Even now,
25 years since junior high,
when Aaron sees teenagers
walking on his side
of the street, he
crosses to the other side,

scared. When his
mother died,
and Aunt Carol said,
"Time will heal you,
dear," he told her go
to Hell. Always

13 years old, Death
makes smart comments—
when it finds you,
you have no other side
to cross over to.

# AARON SEES A GHOST

1.

It's raining.
Faces entering look match-lit.
The first shrieks from hell
unfold in anonymous hotel rooms.
On each floor, the same
magazine heads and cartlike bodies.
The tortured ghost of language
hunts for a hiding place from laughing
windows. All the art
from every century can't reflect
the boredom of coffee tables,
the deafness of lamps
dusted by maids, fixed by houseboys.

2.

In the lobby I remember sitting
in the big apple tree, watching
fruit ripen, fixing
myself among leaves, candles
lighting cracks between seasons,
waking to Everett Dirksen Memorial Marigolds,
brass buttons at dawn.

Bell rings. Someone wants service.
I register the scrawl, straighten

myself like papers
under his left elbow.

I check them in, the strain
of money creasing their faces,
feeling the sympathy
of one who has touched naked flesh
and felt bare bone.
A need to disturb.

3.


Here at the Glen Ellyn Holiday Inn
an elevator lets you out
in heaven or hell.

God, a radio playing
in the bar, his voice
the d.j. working the graveyard shift,
His truth spliced by commercials.

Listen... not an hour is moving.
You hate me when I say "No vacancy."
Pounding your fist you say,
"I'm really mad!"

You wish I would turn off the radio—
you never did like mystics.

4.


Apple blossoms on the apple tree.
Mermaids in the boughs.

Match-lit.

These gray-suited shadows
demand the steak dinner
at the rainbow's end, a woman
to rent like a room.

Lipless boys
recalling their nightmares, checking
their closets for a ghost
I still see so often.

# PORK ROAST

Aaron eats pork roast.
The phone rings—hello,
is this Aaron? Yes.
I'm a friend of Phil McGill's—

you don't know me,
but Phil died Monday—
the service is Thursday
at ten if you'd like
to attend. CLICK.

Phil, lovely light, a firefly,
Aaron thinks as he
goes to the closet,
picks out a black
jacket. Thursday he sits

in a pew. Crying is okay
here, among strangers.

Aaron remembers Phil,
their one night.
 Without thinking,
he feels nodes
on his neck.

# AARON AND PLAGUES

Many circle the funeral home:
 "Jesus, forgive them."
A woman in a tan
coat walks with both
hands open
so Christ will swim into her.

From the paper they know
how Richard got here.
They hold his memory hostage,
a lesson for lost souls
inside: Jesus wipes out millions
when He's angry.

They scream at mourners
entering, admire spit
on their own faces, proof
that God has singled them out
for persecution and Heaven.

 "Repent,"
they say, prayer an assassin
shooting at random,
sure to snuff someone.

# 2. How To Fly

# AARON'S EPITHALAMION

Diane asked me to write
a poem for her wedding.
She's marrying a brunette
whose shoes made little squeaks
when he walked up to the altar.
After I read the poem
stuffed with God, flowers,
and planets,

I began to wish I hadn't—
I kept hearing his shoes
at the reception.
I knew then he'd leave her

but he didn't
until they moved to Santa Fe.
It was her fault,
the Dorcas Circle ladies said—
you have to do everything
for a man, everything.

They sent her letters
she never answered.
They were "concerned"
and said so to their husbands,
blank stares
who actually spoke
sometimes: truths rumbling

in pot bellies under bald heads
they could nod at
before falling asleep.

# AARON CONSIDERS A CEREMONY

I'd like to stand with you
before our friends,
watusi and waltz
the night away. Oh, let's

have one night of bad music
and good promises to say:
love matters,
love is possible,
and if we sound sentimental,
so be it. Because

the world claims us soon enough
with irony and committees.
Will I keep silent
as if in Reading Gaol, not
putting your picture on my desk—

we're always a paycheck away
from homelessness.
So let us have one night,
love, let us have one night.

# DUMPED

Aaron's been dumped again.

Jerry,
Ted,
Phil,
Jim—

the names grew less distinct
after him. Aaron says:

I'm only happy when
in love, sits
in Woody's Bar holding
an unlit cigarette
imitating Bette Davis
in *Now, Voyager*

badly. Now
that Jim's dumped him
("You're too demanding.")
Aaron hangs clothes out
to dry, the sun

winking behind the dumpster
holding any shirt
Jim liked him in.

# SOMETIMES AT A PARTY

Sometimes at a party
Aaron finds that his head
is breaking

dishes thrown by lovers
whose fighting leaves
one bleeding on the floor,

he laughs, carries on
as if this fight
is no closer than tabloid

talk of two film stars,
hops from guest to guest,
cracks jokes,

cracks open
the back door,
slips out,

voices in his head
stopped
only by a blue

browallia
in moonlight's thin
white pajama bottoms.

# AARON'S THREE PLANETARY WISHES

All nine planets rock,
but if I could visit three,
I'd choose Mercury, Uranus,
and Pluto.

Freezing on one side,
boiling on the other,
straddle the line
between Mercury's cold
and heat, are you in

God's mouth? Who bopped
over gas giant Uranus's poles?
Enter a methane, ammoniac
garden growing lethal green
flowers. Pluto

will always be a planet to me.
This tease can crawl
under Neptune's wire fence
to sidle up to the sun.
Pluto's moon Charon,
a stone eye watching.
Vacation over,

I'd pine for blue Earth,
her waters and daylilies,
animals and wallows.

# LEARN HOW TO FLY

Not one to adore the past
(except his own)
Aaron rarely reads
about knights and kings
a few queens maybe
but kings bore him.
Still, he knows
that had he lived in Greece
*then* he'd have given
his heart gladly to Icarus
who fell
and fell
until the sea,
a venus flytrap,
ate him. Aaron wants
to learn how to fly
but would never
go too near the sun—
he hates heat,
prefers rain,
his arm candles,
wax wings,
gliding between clouds,
coastlines, dunes—
the earth,
a stem strong
enough to hold
his descending petal.

# TRASH

Aaron hates going to TRASH
alone. Travis arrives.

Music, a severed head
rolling from dancer to dancer.
Orange handkerchiefs light up
several backsides. One guy slides
his zipper up and down
when his partner sinks to his knees.

Shadows. Brief flickers that leap
and fade. Faintly,
daylight wedges open the sky,
a darting snake tongue: amphibian
crawling between cartops.

# SMOKESCREEN

Enter by a thick black door
into smoke hanging from the ceiling
like rows of gray belts.
Some search for St. Sebastian.
Others map out
construction workers or gas pumpers,
those sunlit shoulders.
Most settle for the hunt, seek
the hole in desire's pocket.

Aaron fidgets
with buttons on his blue shirt, fears
another night alone
or waking with one he hates.
A man in his thirties stalks
from a video game:
"I'll bet you make quick decisions;
you know exactly what you want."
Torn by red and yellow lights,
Aaron says, "Sometimes."
Images multiply in mirrors,
shadows clutch shadows.

Music glows,
a white-hot tip of frantic flame.
The man yanks Aaron to him, stamps
his lips with wet kisses.

Drumbeat hurtles into drumbeat; strobes
flatten like oriental poppy petals.
Nervous, out of cigarettes, Aaron
returns to night air
populated with distant bodies.

At home he undresses behind
a white screen in a room stuffed
with books and art
objects cold as dead young hands.

# SANCTUARY

Jesus it's like sitting at a stoplight at Time's edge.
Phillip says he wishes he didn't feel like winter:
he's a Libra, can't juggle his inner stars.

I smile
into each remark:
conversation
a subway—
cars hurtling
between green faces.

Hand draws toward hand, searching for the safety in numbers
above two, safety snared on barbed wire. A light at the end
of a cigarette. As music turns us to metal, each eyeball
is a still point. Doors liquify. Like dissolving tongues, words
become mist, the last notes of a tune. Lonely shadows
spy on their bodies. I'd like to dance with them, call them
to my bones, let my cells divide in their questions.

Someone is calling.
Someone struck dumb, a huge mouth
sucking me in for food, for air.
No resistance.
Dying lights. Soon I'll be
unable to see
myself.

The Valley of these Shadows. Anyone who has seen
love cresting in smoke is Christ hanging on the cross
words. Believers with sad eyes walled in
by exquisite kisses.

# BUTTERFLY IN SMOKE

White spheres burn above the street
 Hold the summer night to your ear
A blues singer will borrow your decline
 Aaron holds a Newport like Garbo
 showing off a new bracelet
 This Bastille Day is fast
becoming a mystic night dunked
 in a chalice of anonymous black jeans
 Roses float on a table's bones
 petals thin as smoke they turn in
 Again Aaron's on the loose
 The city bobs against his shoulders
Each building ash soft on his jacket
 Unexpected a dark
butterfly trembles in his chest
 Dawn a white wing over a fountain

# SPIDER BREAK-UP

Like a rowboat on a lake
when the breeze kicks up
and slides you to a sandbar.
You look out on yellow

beach-ball colored water
lilies—that's how Steve
drifts into affairs, how
he got messed up with Sean—

two months in, Steve
thought Sean really might be
"the one," though
Sean saying *love* sounded

no different than when
he was ordering
White Castle fries. Steve
couldn't dowse one

memory—how when
they were kids, Sean would
torture spiders, taking a stick
to webs, teasing them out,

goring them. In bed
Steve saw spiders on sheets.
Sean's stick, ready
to come down hard.

# AARON PROMISES HIMSELF
# NEVERNEVER NEVER AGAIN

I love you like a trainwreck
 in southern Alberta
 a flaming red caboose
 the conductor dashing around
 busted luggage open
perfectly pink suspenders
 a stranger blessing it all
 with a magic wand
 saying Jesus is with us when we
 suffer though He's in Heaven
 basking authorities
 show up
 take pictures
to find how it happened
 nobody ever finds out
 just another wreck
 final
 fatal
forgotten

# AARON HEARS KAREN CARPENTER

> "I'm looking for love,
> but it's just not there"
> The Carpenters, 1966

Driving to Lowe's for mini-blinds,
I hear my Carpenters tape.
Strings, oboes. Karen trapped
between chords. Grief pins her.

I didn't like them much
in their heyday but when wounded
birds flutter in my brain, I crave
Karen.

They got angry letters
for "Goodbye To Love,"
the guitar almost
rock n roll. She got so

thin she disappeared, became
a late night monologue joke,
had said goodbye to love—
and to hate.

Her heart literally broke.

# THE SAME

The same day
Aaron read that West Virginia
passed a law
declaring marriage
is a man
and a woman
only, he gets an e-mail
which says,
"My sister-in-law
left her husband,
fled to Massachusetts,
my brother had been
beating her
and ripped out
all the phones."

# LAMPLIGHT

Aaron's stung by whirring bees
of lamplight. Evening opens,
closes like eighteen lips
kissing him. Stars
stagger over Skid Row to talk
by the flophouse where he'll store
his body for the night.

Morning, good for pandering nickels,
dimes, an occasional quarter. Red wine
has turned his knuckles orange.

Afternoon fell against Chicago,
broke its picture window.
He was steam above the river
as pleasure boats rolled into Lake Michigan.
Shouting children went home to his ears
on motorized laughter.

Among hookers, pimps, and other
respectable show-going folk, he
stumbles up stairs, casually walks out
to the moon, looks down at the body
dissolving on the bed in puke.

Stingers of bright lamplight
hiss against his window.

# AARON WOKE UP

I woke up and reveled—
it just couldn't be, how
could I be so lucky:

no sun, the stupid yellow thing
that keeps leaning on my windows,
gone! Still dark by midmorning,
maybe I'll get through
a whole day without one ray on my roof. Some call

themselves "sun worshippers."
Deluded! I can understand those
who worship rain and snow—
but sun? Why? Many even open
their curtains to let sun in.

What a strange time. Others tan,
sit under the sun or
tanning parlor lamps.

Imagine. Wanting the sun
to crawl all over you. What next?

# ONE FLOOR BELOW

Years ago he got used to floating sidewalks and airborne stores. At first he hated them, kept dropping under them, but made peace with that—after all, people can make a world anywhere, even in space. Some of his best friends are planets. Pluto's a great comfort. Jupiter farts too much but is otherwise dependable. He lives one floor below reality. Fine—reality drives an ugly car.

# MAN WITH A BAD BACK

At the 7-11 Aaron
bends to pick up a paper,
drops it around his feet.
"Can't move," he screams,
his face in creases
of pain. "Excuse me,"
another says, pushing
to the coffee machine
Aaron blocks. The clerk
brings him a chair he
slowly drips onto,
seems to revive slightly,
his face returning
from that dark place
where nobody offers a chair
and no machine needs us.

# AARON WATCHING

In the Veterinary Clinic,
a talk show: people
abused in high school
confront their tormentors.

He sits beside a grim black lab
with bloody ears.
Another dog across the room
sits like Queen Elizabeth.
His cats cry in the "container,"
a gray jacket over it
so he can avoid
their terrorized faces.

Some woman on the show
tells of being spat on—

his turn. He bring in the cats,
closes both doors after
entering the examining room.

# LETTER

Dear Willy Jean:

Why am I writing? You'll never answer, having solved
yourself in New Orleans. Perhaps you'll hold the envelope
to the light to check for a signature. If only I had been
bluffing when I said I love you! Even then I could only
utter "love" as if the "I" and "you" were just excess
baggage. Still, I'm sure you got the message. That's when
the new wore off. Communication breakdown. I try to act
modern, to look like people in pop psychology books, but
then, strangely, the sight of a girl eating fish sticks
on a porch or a man clipping a hedge undoes me totally.

 I wish I could say "Goddammit I'm lonely and pissed,"
but all that comes out is some absurd American bulletin:
shirts on sale at Wal-Mart or the first time I heard
"Three Times In Love" on WCBR. Besides, I'm always
imprecise. Just when I'm thinking most kindly of you,
a desire to torture the cat swells up. I felt angry,
but then in Jewel Groceries I burst out laughing
in aisle three trying to decide which oil to buy.
Weeks later, I felt blind among the flowers, going window
shopping on Ardmore Avenue, going to the bank, going mad
with a CD copy of <u>The Blades of Grass Are Not For Smoking</u>.

 Letter writing, I hear, is therapeutic, but I want no
hands laid on me. I could say how "old" I feel since you left,
but it would be a lie. Actually, my inner clock gallops
in reverse! Today I embarrass myself with youth. I can spend
whole hours not remembering.

You have no Achilles heel. If you are edges, I'm
surfaces. I had hoped that opposites attract, but by now
I should be used to the one-way pull, a useless slaughter.
This is the first letter I've written without expecting a reply:
May the sun cut your throat!

Yours,

Aaron Stern

# 3. Vanishing

# AARON SALUTES

America, you old garden party.
You take yourself too seriously
in your deck chairs, clutching
a glass of chablis, saying
you agree
you agree.
And when you were little
you stood by your desk
mouthing the Pledge of Allegiance,
always looking out the window
or at the blackboard.
Older now, you wish
Canada bordered Mexico
and the Bering Sea began at China.
That wouldn't help, would it?
They'd just build a new patio
elsewhere, have the same chats
around faultless flower boxes,
kids repeating the same
promises to distant chalk.

# LOST IN HOME DEPOT

Tormented cars clot
the parking lot. Inside

Aaron hunts a new mower blade.
Products lining deep aisles,
paint thinner and electric
tube goddesses, lure dads.

A guy barks at a kid
in an orange apron:
"Thatch for my lawn chair!"
The grinning kid looks lost,
points. Aaron stops
to mull over screws,

remembers Kranz's Hardware
back in Villa Park where
he grew up, a smell of wood
and galoshes, finds his blade,
cuts to the checkout, holds
a VISA card like it's his
dad's hand, walks out into

wet gray. He's in love,
works, has a garden. Here
he looks both ways—

a dark puddle, harsh wind. Cars
leap at anyone who tries

to get free, circle the lot,
exit, a stoplight's red
eye glaring.

# AARON IN PARAGUAY

Why am I here?
No sea, no midnight sun
on my shoulders, a pink
phlox coat.

A rough arrival. Hotel pests
skitter up my dreams.
The bellhop sees me
as a frog in an experiment.

When it rains I'd love
to run out dancing. I miss
dahlias scrunched
by my door at home.

I will say this for Paraguay:
I am just a guy natives see
walking—I've heard
nobody call me crazy
for muttering in my sleeves.

# AARON AT A BORDER

When he and I are
in bed we are at
a border:

we surrender gender
though no one's here
to ensure that we're
on the level. We're never
on the level—always fluid,
we move in many
directions at once. When

we touch, we burst

in joy we roil in,

the ooze and lick of love.

# THE SMALL DEATH

Aaron Stern in a dark restaurant
drinking. Two men who make him sigh
are bored—an Aussie lady
keeps winking at the guy

on Aaron's left side
but he only has eyes for Jack
sitting on Aaron's right side, lumped
in gym shorts: provocative sack.

The waiter, what a monolith,
something booted out of Stonehenge.
Aaron's trying to catch his eye;
they've caught Montezuma's Revenge.

Pete and Jack share a delux suite.
They look like tourists: calypso
music accompanies voodoo.
They leave the brown door ajar

so passersby can see them screwing.
The rich always do as they please,
except for Aaron, hot, alone,
masturbating behind tall trees.

# AARON IN TRINIDAD

I wish America had never been
discovered. Leave these islands

to spice-bushes
and plume flowers. Maybe
it's because I'm an orphan.
America, an endless family reunion.
Everywhere you go,
someone shoves a cocktail
in your hand and says:
Where have you been?
What are you doing now?
Where are we going—your place

or mine? I'm not going anywhere.
I'm content to wade
in the waters off Port-Au-Spain,
sky before me, tar pits
behind me.

Today I heard the awful news:
Alvin Barker is dead.
Mrs. McFrunt sent a cable
in case I should like to attend
the funeral. I couldn't possibly
leave this beach but I will
collect dead jellies and give
a eulogy to blue tentacles.
Alvin would have liked that.

Among chanting Hindus
and the frozen light bulbs
of Catholic eyes, I shall send
him on his way: gentle
electron floating in the ionosphere.

# OH DEAR

In the church basement he sees
the groom and the best man kissing.
20 minutes before the ceremony.

They wave at him. He thinks that surely
this marriage will be up in flames
quickly yet these unions can go
on and on. Secrets stack up
like cereal boxes bought on sale.
Sometimes they pour out,
but by then it doesn't matter so much.
Doctor's appointments. Joint returns.
Grandchildren visiting.

Thirty years ago in Philosophy class
he studied The Mind-Body Problem.
It's still a problem. Maybe
the Mind and Body have separate bedrooms—
no one has to block out bad snoring.

Morning comes. The doors open.
Two pieces of toast, one buttered.

# BURNING SILVER PEARS

Moonlight on
The Horner Monument Company,
a white chisel hunting a name.

Fun Millicent says,
"Aaron, let's go to the cemetery."
We race down hills in the road,
a roller coaster in our guts.
A redbud flash, lightning
rooted in the parkway.
When we see the cemetery,
I say hello to bones
which have shed each leaf
of any former meanness.
Millicent's overcome
with gratitude—every blossom,
every bit of bark—our kind
beneath us sweetening mulch.
We leave. Homes

line the road—chimneys
shovel smoke into star pockets
bulging with burning silver pears.

# AARON PEERS INTO THE DARKNESS OF FLOWERS

Hold it right there! Do you
see flowers as benevolent deities?
Flowers are spooky. Roots crawl
toward the open eye

ball in the Earth's center.
Death walks with flowers,
kisses whatever withers.

Putting flowers around our dead,
that's weird. Or is it?
Blossoms, gatekeepers
to ground we get dumped into—
darkness overtakes everything.

A shine comes. The moon picks
one tiny flower
to turn tides with.

# VALVES

Maybe the soul can close
its valves like stone.
Mine will take a rowboat
into a bay where orioles
do orange jigs, frogs crumple
lily pads and leaves
fall in each other's dreams.

Owls go there. Talons
seize the night.

You won't be able to find
my soul. His attention valves,
closed. You might mistake him
for mica. Then he can be alone,

skin flaking with quiet.

# WHAT VANISHES

In Kapustan people fear hills
so much, they won't enter houses
with stairs. Everything must be flat.
Aaron would like that—no hills,
no mountains! Why climb
closer to the sun's

jaundiced eye? Take him
where miles never tip
or tumble. Back home we lose
what comes into view when the road
tilts up and away—

we head out toward what
vanishes.

# AARON WITHOUT MIRRORS

I remove my last mirror.

At the gym,
mirrors follow me.
I memorize the floor.
Others hold barbells:
models who leap from a page,
begin breathing at iron's touch.

Picture windows lock me
in glass,
an ant in candlewax.

The scariest mirrors?
A lover's eyes.
A child's eyes.
No choice but to see
myself. Only

Death, an absence
of mirrors. We buzz
in Earth's hive,
 the atom a house
with many rooms,

the tiny soul,
a place too small
to give a reflection.

# RINSE AND SPIT

Told to rinse
and spit, my blood
stains white porcelain.
 In no position

to argue, I recline and
let him finish me.
The Bee Gees sing
"Too Much Heaven"
on a radio. Will Heaven
have floss, waiting rooms,
*Time*? Maybe

it will have blood.
Without blood there's
little hope for sex.
Some say in heaven
we lack bodies
so we don't desire—
heaven, a TV plugged
into God, perfect

reception, tingles
of static electricity,
scentless.

# RESTING IN PEACE

When my love and I
hold each other after
making love, oh

then I am at peace.
He is tender and time
feels softer, like a peony.

We know the world throws
tantrums beyond the bed,
can hear lawnmowers,

cars backfiring, the trash can
cats just overturned. We
also hear our hearts

beating. How lovely
drifting off and not
saying even one word.

Legs entangled, perhaps
our sprawl looks funny. Peace
is funny like that—

it winds around us
as we wind around
each other.

# BOTCHED BEGINNINGS

For Sir Stephen Spender

Aaron, the last kid to learn
left from right, last
to quit training wheels,
last to learn directions.

Getting lost,
a way of life, not

so bad. He gets into places
others don't. In church,
lost sheep Aaron got
found by God, slipped free.
People wrapped him in maps
it took years to squirm out of.

Wherever he starts
he won't stop—the dream
of arrival, a nightmare. He spent
years angling for a destination.
Exhausted, he sped down

weird roads, met trees
whose leaves pointed him onward.
He's ready to start again,
a wheezy directional sense,

the horizon a witch
inviting him to join her
in some dive of a sky.

# FINISH LINE

I grew up needing
finish lines. Win or lose,
yes, no,
Yankees 4 Bluejays 3.
Nothing's worked out

that way. I was told
heaven's a finish line:
lay my grief down
at the cross,
get a crown—do I
want to be regal

for eternity? Flowers
open. Close.
Then the long ache
underground,
waiting
to begin again,
to start fresh.